GW01374775

THIS JOURNAL BELONGS TO:

____

Printed in Great Britain
by Amazon

74823502R00119